Short Skits for Youth Ministry

by Chuck Bolte and Paul McCusker

Loveland, Colorado

Note

The price of this text includes the right for you to make as many copies of the skits as you need for your immediate youth group. If another church or organization wants copies of these skits, it must purchase *Short Skits for Youth Ministry* in order to receive performance rights.

Short Skits for Youth Ministry

Credits

Edited by Michael Warden
Cover designed by Liz Howe
Cover photography by David Priest

Library of Congress Cataloging-in-Publication Data
Bolte, Chuck, 1950-
    Short skits for youth ministry / by Chuck Bolte and Paul McCusker.
       p.   cm.
    Includes index.
    ISBN 1-55945-173-4
    1. Drama in Christian education. 2. Christian drama, American.
3. Church work with youth. I. McCusker, Paul, 1958-   .
II. Title.
BV1534.4.B625 1993
246'.7—dc20   93-11233
                                                           CIP

12 11 10 9 8 7 6 5   04 03 02 01 00 99 98 97

Printed in the United States of America.

Contents

Introduction

"Excuse me. Are you listening?"

Have you ever used that line in a youth group meeting? a Bible study? a group devotional? That's okay. Just about every youth worker has let those words flutter off his or her tongue at one time or another while working with kids. It's not uncommon.

But while we're spending so much time trying to get kids to listen to us, are we spending enough time listening to them? to what their lack of attention might be telling us?

"Lectures are boring."

"This stuff has nothing to do with real life."

"I'm tired of just sitting and staring at the floor—I want to *do* something."

Okay, so kids want more action. And they want to know how the issues you're talking about really affect their lives—*really*. And they don't want lectures.

How do you accomplish all that and still manage to direct kids toward the truths you want them to grasp? Clearly, you need a resource that gets kids actively involved, challenges them to openly discuss issues in their lives, and helps them find solutions out of their faith in God. Is there such a thing in the universe?

Well, actually, you're holding it.

Short Skits for Youth Ministry contains 30 fast, hot-topic skits that draw kids into an issue or truth on more than just an intellectual level. The objective of these skits is to say as much as possible in as little time as possible. This makes the skits easy to use while still packing a significant punch for discussion. And the best part is there's no need for preparation time. Just assign parts and have kids create their characters right on the spot.

About the Skits

The skits were created with specific goals in mind. First, they're brief "snapshots" of particular topics, characters, and situations familiar to your group. The topics vary from current "controversial" issues, such as premarital sex and cheating, to practical, everyday concerns, such as family communication and money.

The skits don't presume to cover every aspect of a topic, nor do they give neatly packaged answers. They're more like active, involving discussion-starters. They open the door to an issue; it's up to you and your group to see where each skit leads.

Second, these skits can be performed almost anywhere at any time. Thus, you won't see much elaboration on specific settings or acting requirements. Two chairs can be a living room, a park bench, or a tree limb. Imagination is the key.

For kids who aren't interested in drama for drama's sake, these skits can be simple, innovative activities to introduce a topic. For others who have more theatrical tendencies, these dramatic snippets can be combined into a series for a variety show. In addition, the skits can be used in the worship service as sermon-enhancers or in the mall as outreach dramas. This handy little resource can really help your group members grow in their faith.

About the Technical Directions

Certain terms in the dialogue may be unfamiliar to some who haven't studied drama. The most commonly used notation found here is the *(Pause)*. A pause is exactly that: a momentary stop in the flow of dialogue allowing the character (or the audience) to think, take action, or react to what's happening. Exactly how long a pause lasts depends on the character, dialogue, and situation. By using pauses effectively, your would-be actors can heighten the drama or draw bigger laughs.

The characters in these skits are often on stage when the skit begins and ends. In these cases, simply ask the actors to freeze in position before beginning. When the skit ends, have the actors freeze (so everyone knows the skit is over) and then walk away while you lead into the discussion.

About Having Fun

Believe it or not, your kids watch you. That's why when it comes to these skits, your wholehearted participation is imperative. Take part in the skits once in a while. And when you're on the side-lines, pay attention to the action on stage. Become involved with it, right along with your kids. If you do, you'll gain the unique pleasure of discovering truths about life with them.

You can try something new, innovative, and fun with your kids and use these skits. Or you can stay on familiar ground and stick with the stuff you're already doing. It's up to you.

Skits

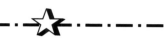

The Accused

Topic: *Sharing faith*

The Scene

Two teenagers fear they might be accused of a "crime" that their friend has committed.

Characters

JASON
ADAM
ADULT (off-stage voice)

★★★

(This sketch can involve two males or two females plus an off-stage male or female voice. Simply change the names of the characters. For the purpose of this sketch, we will use two males, Jason and Adam. Their conversation takes place inside a courtroom so they're speaking in loud whispers.)

JASON   *(Disturbed)* Oh man . . .

ADAM   I knew if he wasn't careful he'd get caught.

JASON   Yeah, well Josh isn't known for his subtlety.

ADAM   Anybody with half a brain never would've gotten into this mess.

JASON   What does that make *us*, huh? *We're* in the middle of it now.

ADAM   What do you mean "we"? They didn't call *me* to testify against him! And if they did, I'd tell 'em that I didn't have anything to do with it.

JASON   What? You're one of Josh's best friends. At one point you were *totally* involved in the whole thing.

ADAM   Yeah, well if you decide to say that on the witness stand, I'll deny it. Nobody can prove anything.

JASON   You're gonna let Josh take the rap alone?

ADAM   Hey, if he's dumb enough to get arrested, why not? You think I wanna go to jail just for *him?* Forget it. *(Pause.)* So what are you gonna say?

JASON   *(Pausing, thoughtfully)* I don't know. *(Pause.)* The truth, I guess.

ADAM   *(Shocked)* You're crazy! They'll nail you, too!

JASON   *(Pause.)* I know.

ADAM   You're off your rocker!

JASON   Maybe. But what bugs me is that even if I do confess, I'm not sure they'll have enough evidence to convict me.

ADAM   That *bugs* you?!

JASON   Yeah.

ADULT   *(Off stage)* All rise. The honorable Judge Lawrence Edwards presiding. The case...the State vs. Joshua Allen. Mr. Allen is accused of being a Christian. The state contends that there is ample evidence of such and seeks to prosecute him under the current laws of this land...

Discussion Starters

1. What did you think of the twist at the end of this skit? Explain. Though the ending may seem a bit outrageous, do you think there would be enough evidence to publicly convict you of being a Christian? Why or why not?

2. What kind of evidence of faith should a Christian exhibit? Explain.

3. Read 1 John 2:23. How does this Scripture relate to this skit and to our responsibility to share our faith as Christians?

The Advance

— · — · — · — · — · — ☆ — · — · — · — · — · —

Topic: *Money*

The Scene

A teenage daughter (or son) asks her father for an advance on her allowance.

Characters

FATHER
DAUGHTER (or son)

★★★

(A home. Father is sitting, reading.)

DAUGHTER   *(Entering)* Dad can I have my allowance?

FATHER   No.

DAUGHTER   Oh, come on. Please? Just an advance?

FATHER   Which advance is this: The advance against next week's allowance that I advanced to you two weeks ago—or an advance on the following week's allowance that you borrowed the day before yesterday?

DAUGHTER   I don't care. You can call it whatever advance you want.

FATHER   You're missing the point.

DAUGHTER   I need it, Dad. It's important.

FATHER   I'm sure.

DAUGHTER   Seriously! I have to pay back some money I borrowed at school. My life won't be worth a penny otherwise.

FATHER   Now wait a minute...after I've given you all those advances you still borrowed money from someone at school?

DAUGHTER Well, the shortest version of the story is—yes.

FATHER But *why?* Where is all your money going?

DAUGHTER Different things. I don't know. Please, Dad?

FATHER No, Jamie. I won't do it. You have to learn how to use your money wisely.

DAUGHTER But that's not fair! Nobody else in America has to do that!

FATHER Save the social commentary for a debate class. No advance.

DAUGHTER But...but if I don't go into debt, how will I establish a good credit line? What will I do when I get older? I won't be able to buy a car...or a house! You want to see your only child destitute?

FATHER I'd like to see my only daughter use her money wisely.

DAUGHTER Okay. Never mind. I only borrowed the money to get you a surprise birthday gift.

FATHER *(Pause.)* How much did you borrow?

DAUGHTER Ten bucks.

FATHER *(Pulling out wallet, handing her a bill)* Here's $20. But I still expect you to learn to use money wisely.

DAUGHTER I thought buying you a gift was the wisest thing I could do. *(She kisses him on the cheek and exits.)*

FATHER *(Resuming his reading)* Good answer.

Discussion Starters

1. What advice would you give to this daughter about her spending? Should the father have given his daughter money? Why or why not?

2. What do you think about the daughter's statements about American attitudes toward money: overspending and needing to borrow for credit? Do you think God approves of that way of handling money? Why or why not? What choices can we make as Christians not to become trapped in the consumer "system"?

3. Do you receive an allowance of any sort from your parents? If so, how did you come to an arrangement about the amount? Would you make a similar arrangement with your own children? Why or why not?

Authority

---⭐---

Topic: *Authority*

The Scene

A teenager talks to his youth leader about the difficulty he has following someone he doesn't respect.

Characters

DAVE
YOUTH LEADER

★★★

(Dave is seated, talking to his youth leader.)

DAVE   *(Upset)* The guy is a total jerk.

LEADER   Who?

DAVE   Reeves . . . my history teacher.

LEADER   Why do you say that?

DAVE   Because he gave me an incomplete on my last paper.

LEADER   Was it?

DAVE   Incomplete? Yeah, but I didn't know it when I turned it in. He added the requirement to include a bibliography when I was out sick.

LEADER   Has he done anything else that you don't like?

DAVE   It's not just what he's done, it's his attitude. He's definitely got something against me.

LEADER   What do you mean?

DAVE   If Derrick didn't have a bibliography in *his* report, I guarantee you that *he* wouldn't have gotten an incomplete. It's all a matter of who in the class kisses up to him.

LEADER What kinds of things does Derrick do to "kiss up to" Mr. Reeves?

DAVE Oh, you know, stuff like always calling him *Mr.* Reeves and asking questions during class. He knows that Reeves *loves* that kind of treatment. And because of that, Derrick can do no wrong.

LEADER Hmm...that's funny.

DAVE What?

LEADER Well, Derrick just told me that Mr. Reeves gave *him* a bad grade on a term paper, too.

DAVE It must have been a freak accident. I'm telling you, the guy deserves no respect.

LEADER Well, maybe he *isn't* a great instructor, but it doesn't change the fact that he *is* the teacher.

DAVE Hey, just 'cause a guy has a title doesn't mean I've got to give him some kind of special treatment.

LEADER Really...well, how 'bout last summer at camp when you were a cabin counselor. Maybe you didn't expect any "special treatment" from those kids, but you sure expected them to do what you asked...because *you* were the counselor. *(Pause.)* Right?

DAVE *(Pausing, thinking, hesitantly)* Yeah, I guess. But *I* wasn't a jerk about it.

LEADER True. But you didn't do everything right, either. Remember that time you took the kids out on the nature hike and got lost? Or when you decided to get the campfire going a little quicker by dousing it with gasoline?

DAVE Hey, it worked.

LEADER Yeah, but you all looked pretty silly walking around with no eyebrows. And you still expected the kids to respect your authority after that, didn't you?

DAVE *(Pause.)* All right, I get your point. I'll show Reeves some respect.

LEADER *Mr.* Reeves.

DAVE   Right. *(Pause.)* Let's get out of here. I've gotta study for a history test.

(They exit.)

Discussion Starters

1. Have you ever had a teacher or other authority figure that you had trouble following? Explain. How did you deal with the problem?

2. What specific kinds of actions and attitudes show disrespect to those in authority? What attitudes and actions show respect?

3. Read Romans 13:1-6. Do you think this Scripture refers only to leaders in government? Why or why not?

4. What if someone in authority asks or requires you to do something you think is wrong? Does the Bible require that we do what they say? Why or why not?

A Boring Read

---⋆---

Topic: *The Bible*

The Scene

One teenage guy thinks the Bible is boring to read, but another sees it through different eyes.

Characters

PAUL
PHIL

★★★

(Phil and Paul are sitting in the den. Paul is excitedly describing the contents of a book he's holding.)

PAUL   This thing is unbelievable!

PHIL   That good, huh?

PAUL   Good? It's great! I mean, it's got everything...lots of blood and gore, sex, slimy bad guys, and cool superheroes. I mean, some of the guys in here make the Terminator *(or current popular superhero)* look like Pee Wee Herman *(or "a wimp")*.

PHIL   Sounds like they ought to make a movie out of it.

PAUL   I think they've tried a couple of times, but it didn't come off as good as the book.

PHIL   So...what part are you reading right now?

PAUL   Well, this one guy who is an assistant to the governor has ticked off the governor's wife because she put the moves on him, but he wouldn't have sex with her. Anyway, he gets away, but she claims that he tried to rape her so she gets him arrested and tossed in jail. I'm at the part where the governor is trying to decide what to do with this guy since, up to this point, the governor trusted him.

PHIL Cool! Can I read that part when you're done with it?

PAUL Sure...as a matter of fact, here...take the whole book.

PHIL *(Surprised)* You're kidding!? Hey, thanks.

PAUL It's no big thing. I think we've got six copies at my house.

PHIL Six copies! *(Laughing)* What, is your whole family reading it?

PAUL No, my folks never touch it. The copies are buried somewhere in our library.

PHIL The cover's torn off this one. What's it called?

PAUL The Bible.

Discussion Starters

1. The Bible is filled with many incredible stories. Why do you think most people feel like it is "a boring read"?

2. Do you think people should read the Bible regularly? Why or why not?

3. What are some ways you could make the Bible more exciting to read?

Here are a couple of suggestions:

● Start by setting aside only a few minutes (perhaps five) to read the Bible each day.

● Choose a soundtrack from your favorite action film (like from the Indiana Jones films) and play it in the background while you read (especially passages from the Old Testament).

● Have a friend do the same thing so you can talk about what you've been reading and at the same time, hold each other accountable.

The Breakup

Topic: *Love*

The Scene

Two young men are talking about the breakup of a relationship.

Characters

PERRY
ROBERT

★★★

(Two young men in conversation. This could take place anywhere two young men might feel comfortable to talk freely.)

PERRY   Hold on, Bob. Are you telling me you and Cindy broke up?

ROBERT   Yep. Looks like it.

PERRY   But I don't get it. You two have been together forever. What happened?

ROBERT   *(Shrugging)* I don't know. Something changed. I...I can't explain it.

PERRY   *(Skeptically)* Come on...

ROBERT   It...it's just been the same old thing for us. Nothing new, nothing different. We used to go out and have a good time. But now all we do is sit around her house and watch television and get bored and talk about school and well...

PERRY   Well, what?

ROBERT   I don't know...it's like we were *married* or something.

PERRY   Man, that's a drag. I can't believe it. I can't. You and Cindy breaking up. I thought you loved her.

ROBERT   I did! But it, you know, *changed*. I feel different now. I mean, it's not like I could help it . . .

(They freeze in position.)

Discussion Starters

1. Describe love in your own words (particularly as it pertains to a man and a woman). What are your expectations of love? How does it "feel"?

2. Compare your own description of love with the description you might receive from the following: popular songs, television soap operas, television situation-comedies, and movies.

3. In the sketch, Robert refers to feelings of love changing. What do you think he meant? Have you ever felt like you were in love and weren't? If it wasn't love, what was it?

4. The Bible presents a number of illustrations of love—love for each other (John 15:12), love for God (Deuteronomy 6:5), love by God (John 3:16), love from God (1 Corinthians 13), love between a man and a woman (Song of Solomon; Ephesians 5:22-33), and love between friends (David and Jonathan in 1 Samuel 18 and onward), to name a few. What do these illustrations of love have in common? How are they different? In any of these illustrations, do you detect anything resembling the "feelings" Robert referred to? If yes, where do you see it? If no, what might you conclude about the "spark" with regard to the Bible's view of love?

5. Robert attributes his loss of love for Cindy to feeling and acting like they were married. What did he mean? What does this say about Robert's attitude toward marriage? What are your attitudes about marriage and what it's like?

Change

------------------☆------------------
Topic: *Marriage*

The Scene
Two young women discuss an engagement and a potential problem with the future spouse.

Characters
NICOLE
JANICE

★★★

(The scene could take place anywhere two young women would feel comfortable talking—which is exactly what Nicole and Janice are doing.)

NICOLE So we went home and told my parents.

JANICE Nicole...I'm shocked. You're not even out of high school yet. What about college? What about your *life?*

NICOLE You sound like my parents. We're not going to get married next week or anything. Probably in a couple of years.

JANICE *(Dazed)* Wow. This is gonna take some getting used to. You and Brad...engaged.

NICOLE What's wrong? You don't approve?

JANICE I didn't say that.

NICOLE Well? What *are* you saying?

JANICE *(Trying hard to be diplomatic)* It's just that...I've been around you two and...being engaged is pretty serious stuff. I wouldn't want you to, you know, make a mistake.

NICOLE Janice. Quit stalling. Do you have a problem?

JANICE   Well...it seems like you and Brad fight a lot. I've been worried about it, that's all.

NICOLE   Oh, come on. Those aren't fights. It's just me nagging him about little things he does that annoy me.

JANICE   Really?

NICOLE   Oh yeah. We never fight about anything really big. It's all right.

JANICE   *(Skeptically)* Uh-huh.

NICOLE   Sure. Once we get married, he'll change.

(The two characters freeze.)

Discussion Starters

1. Think about Nicole's attitude about her relationship with her future spouse. Do you think they'll have a happy marriage? Why or why not? How would you counsel her about the relationship?

2. How does the last line of the skit reflect attitudes about potential spouses and marriage? Have you ever tried to make someone change to please you? Did that person change? Why or why not? Can we ever count on other people to change the way we hope they will? Why or why not?

3. How can couples best prepare for a marriage relationship? Someone once speculated that the best question to ask yourself prior to making a commitment in marriage is "Could you spend the rest of your life with this person if he or she never changed for the rest of your life?" React to that question. Is it a fair guide to determine whether you should marry someone? Why or why not?

4. Read Genesis 2:24 and Mark 10:9. How do these passages shed new light on Nicole's view of marriage?

Compassion

---☆---

Topic: *World hunger*

The Scene

A girl is confronted with the need to help the needy.

Characters

SUSAN
LEANNE

★★★

(LeAnne and Susan have just turned off the television.)

SUSAN   This is depressing. Why did *I* have to get this assignment?

LEANNE   Because you chose it.

SUSAN   Oh . . . yeah. Well, it's still depressing. How can those people live like that?

LEANNE   Well I don't think they all got together and said, "Gee, what say we all starve to death?" Their country hasn't had any rain for nine months.

SUSAN   Why don't they just dig a well or something? If I were living there I never would've let it get that bad for *my* family. I would've moved.

LEANNE   *(Sarcastically)* Gosh, why didn't *they* think of that?

SUSAN   No, I'm serious. I'm tired of every couple of years hearing about some country in the middle of nowhere who can't feed their bazillion starving people. Then, to make things worse, they send newspeople over to take pictures of all those skinny little kids just to get us all to work up enough guilt to give them our hard-earned money.

LEANNE   Oh, so then you *are* giving some of your "hard-earned" money to help?

SUSAN   Well, no . . . anyway, the little bit I could afford to give wouldn't save anybody's life.

LEANNE   Each day when you buy lunch at school or when you go to the mall and get a soda, how much do you usually spend?

SUSAN   I don't know. Probably around a dollar. But if you're suggesting I give it all up just to help some kid I'll never meet, forget it.

LEANNE   No, actually I was going to suggest you just give a *part* of it. I set aside just 65 cents a day, and then at the end of the month I send it in. That little bit not only pays for food, it also covers the costs of some clothes and an education for Makweeboo.

SUSAN   Makweeboo? What's that?

LEANNE   It's not a "what." It's a "who." *(She reaches in her purse or pocket, pulls out a photo, and shows it to Susan.)* She's 9 years old.

SUSAN   *(Smiling)* She's cute!

LEANNE   *(Smiling)* I even got a letter from her this past year letting me know that she became a Christian.

SUSAN   *(Surprised)* You actually hear from her?

LEANNE   Occasionally. But even if I didn't, I'd still send the money. Just having her photo helps me picture her being fed and taken care of. Even though I can't help everyone who is hungry, I can help one.

SUSAN   Sixty-five cents a day, huh? *(Sincerely)* Where do I sign up?

(LeAnne smiles and points to the back of the photo she has as if referring to information on it. They freeze.)

Discussion Starters

1. What do you feel when you see news reports on television about starvation and people in need? Explain.

2. Read aloud Matthew 25:31-46. As Christians, should we have any unique sense of responsibility for those in need? How can we as a group help people in need in other countries? in our own country? in our own neighborhood?

3. Talk with your group about the possibility of sponsoring a child through Compassion International (Box 7000, Colorado Springs, CO 80933) or another similar organization. Then raise the necessary funds and do it!

Family Communication

Topic: *Family communication*

The Scene

Four family members talk about their frustration over each other's lack of understanding.

Characters

DAUGHTER   **MOTHER**
SON   **FATHER**

★★★

(A father, mother, 17-year-old son, and 15-year-old daughter are standing in a diamond shape, facing the audience. Each speaks to the audience as if the others are not present.)

DAUGHTER   I don't know what it takes to get their attention, but it's like my mom and dad are on another planet. They really believe they're the only ones in this family with any kind of pressure on them. I go to school, and the first person I see is Scott. He still hasn't taken the hints I've been dropping that it's over between us. So I duck into the restroom to avoid him, and I bump into Michelle who's ticked because I borrowed her new blouse and haven't returned it yet. So I promise her I'll bring it to school tomorrow (if I remember). I'm already late to class so I fly out into the hallway and run into Jason Prentice . . . literally. So there I am lying on my back with the major hunk of the century standing over me laughing. He offers to help me up, but I'm too embarrassed to even talk. Of course my face is completely red, which makes this mega-zit on my chin look like a volcano trying to erupt. I apologize for being such a geek and crawl off to my math class. I'm late. Mr. Gluckheimer not only notices but decides to make me an example by giving me an additional homework assignment...I have to calculate the circumference of a molecule using a yardstick. This guy should give up his day job and go work at the Comedy Club. So, on top of all that, I walk in the door, and the first thing out of my mom's mouth is "I noticed you didn't do the dishes last night," and my dad gives this kind of knowing grunt. The perfect end for a perfect day.

SON   I hate football. Well actually, I don't hate football, I just hate the coach. The guy is mental. I swear, until I met him I always believed evolution was just a *theory*. He has a favorite play. It's called toss me the ball and have every guy over 250 pounds jump on me. He keeps telling me it will toughen me up...which, of course, is why I look like a jelly doughnut. So I put up with this abuse all week knowing that at least there's a game this weekend. Friday night rolls around and, to my shock, the coach puts me in the game. To his shock, I scored. But are my folks there? Take a wild guess. That's the story of my life. I do good, and nobody notices. So what's the point? Why bother even talking about it?

MOTHER   What am I supposed to do? I try to communicate to my family, and they look at me like I've got four heads and just invented a yet-to-be-discovered language. I know Julie's bugged about something, but she just holds it inside. *(Realizing her own problem)* I suppose we're *all* getting good at that. Jim and I don't talk much anymore. When do we have time? We both have to work to make ends meet, and I still have to maintain house and home. *(Pause.)* All I want to do is "connect," even a little bit, with my family. I don't think it's asking too much to expect the kids to tell me what's on their minds. I ask how their day was, and I get such complex answers as "all right," "okay," and the ever popular "fine." I mean, how can I help them if they don't tell me what's going on?

FATHER   The pressure at work is unreal. I've got quotas to meet, letters to answer, people to manage, bosses to contend with, and customers to satisfy. I don't think I ask for much. I'd just like to be able to come home and not feel like I left one major agenda at the office only to be greeted by another *unspoken* one here. I know how to run a business...I just can't seem to get through to my wife and kids. *(Pausing, thoughtfully)* To be honest, most of the time I feel too tired to even care. But I do love my family. I want to be a great husband and father. I just wish it didn't feel like every time I walked through the door I was stepping into a field of land mines. But I suppose that's wishful thinking. I just want my family to talk to me, not at me...and maybe even try to understand the pressure I'm under. Is that too much to ask?

(They all turn inward toward each other and say the following lines <u>simultaneously</u>.)

**SON,
DAUGHTER,
MOTHER,
FATHER** Hi. How ya doin'? Fine. Good.

(With that, they all turn and exit.)

Discussion Starters

1. On a scale of 1 to 10 (10 being "perfect") how would you rate your family's ability to communicate? What keeps your family from "scoring" higher?

2. Who in your family is best at letting their thoughts and feelings be known? Who is worst?

3. Is specific time ever set aside for you to have family conferences— time to share with everyone in the family updates on your activities, thoughts, and frustrations? Why or why not?

4. Read Ephesians 6:1-4. How do these verses apply to the way families should communicate?

Fanatic

---★---

Topic: *Dating*

The Scene

A change in the relationship between a boyfriend and girlfriend is the center of a conversation between two girls.

Characters

BRIDGET
YOLANDA

★★★

(A place where two girls can talk privately—around a table or sitting casually.)

BRIDGET   So, what's going on with you and Matt? I haven't seen you two together for...days.

YOLANDA   He's mad at me. I don't know what I'm going to do.

BRIDGET   What's the problem?

YOLANDA   *(Pause.)* You know the pastor has been preaching that series about Christian living.

BRIDGET   Yeah?

YOLANDA   Matt and I decided to take it seriously.

BRIDGET   Meaning?

YOLANDA   Oh, like we started studying our Bibles together...and praying together...and I really felt different. Not only about God but...Matt, too.

BRIDGET   Good different or bad different?

YOLANDA   I thought it was good. The more we prayed and studied, the more I wanted our Christianity to be part of...of *everything.* So we started getting real picky about the kinds of movies we went to see and...and places we went and...

BRIDGET   Uh-huh.

YOLANDA   Well, I didn't feel right about what we did when we were, you know, alone together. So, today I told Matt.

BRIDGET   Told him what?

YOLANDA   That I didn't want us to do that sort of thing anymore.

BRIDGET   And what did Matt say?

YOLANDA   He called me a fanatic. *(Pausing, sadly)* I think he wants to break up with me. What am I going to do?

(They freeze.)

Discussion Starters

1. Is Yolanda a fanatic? Why or why not? Based on this sketch, what is your assessment of Matt? Should he break up with Yolanda? Why or why not? Though we don't have the specifics, how do you think Yolanda should have communicated her concerns to Matt?

2. Apart from sexual sin, how might differences be created between two people as they grow as Christians? How can such differences be resolved? Can one Christian "outgrow" another? How can one Christian encourage or stimulate another Christian in his or her Christian growth?

3. Read 1 John 1:9; 1 Corinthians 6:11; 2 Corinthians 5:17; 1 Corinthians 10:13; and 2 Peter 2:9. How can you apply these verses to your life? to your relationship with others?

"Geek Search"

- - ☆ - -

Topic: *Judging others*

The Scene

Three people compete on a game show to see who is the biggest geek.

Characters

ANNOUNCER   FRED McMAYHEM
HEATHER (Guest)   BUD (Contestant)
BUFFY (Guest)   LUKE (Guest)
JERRY (Contestant)   WALK-ON SPEAKER
SUSAN (Contestant)

★★★

(The announcer is off stage. Three contestants are seated, facing the audience in a typical game show setting. Opposite them are the panel of guests who will question the contestants. Joining them is the equally typical game show host standing to one side.)

ANNOUNCER   *(Off stage)* It's time for...\"Geek Search"!!! Everybody's favorite game show where young people from across the country compete to see who *really is* the biggest geek on the planet. And here's your host for "Geek Search," Fred McMayhem!

FRED   *(Entering)* Thank you...Thanks very much and welcome to this week's "Geek Search," where young people from across the country...

ANNOUNCER   *(Off stage)* I already said that.

FRED   Right. Well, Johnny, let's meet our contestants.

ANNOUNCER   *(Off stage)* Fred, our first contestant calls *(fill in the name of your rival high school or town)* home. He's hopeless when it comes to hand-eye coordination and couldn't hit a baseball if it was the size of a cruise ship...here's Bud Tutwinkle.

(Audience applause.)

ANNOUNCER   *(Off stage)* Our next contestant hails from *(again, give the name of your rival high school or town).* She's short and highly unattractive...meet Susan Slumppumper.

(Audience applause.)

ANNOUNCER   *(Off stage)* Last, and perhaps least, is a young man— at least I believe he's a man—whose most endearing quality is his ability to pick both nostrils, simultaneously, with his index and pinky fingers...pray for, Jerry Mander.

(Audience applause.)

FRED   Thanks, Johnny, and a special welcome to all the contestants and to our distinguished panel of guests. Well-groomed and pretty doggone impressive, let's welcome Heather, Luke, and Buffy!

(Audience applause.)

FRED   Heather, let's begin with you. Choose your contestant and fire away!

HEATHER   All right, I think I'll begin with Todd Butwinkle...

BUD   That's *Bud Tut*winkle.

HEATHER   Whatever. We know you can't tie your shoe without falling over, and you look like death eating a cracker. In light of that, can you tell this panel what *positive* attributes you have...if any?

BUD   Well, I enjoy reading...

BUFFY   *(Cutting him off)* There's a shocker.

BUD   ...and I like to work with the mentally handicapped.

LUKE   In your case, isn't that like being *self-employed?*

(Heather, Luke, and Buffy laugh.)

FRED   All right, let's move on to contestant #2, Susan Slumppumper. And let's begin our questioning with Luke.

LUKE   So, tell me, Susan, when *was* the last time you got a phone call from someone other than your mother?

(Panelists laugh again.)

HEATHER   Yeah, and what cemetery did you steal the outfit from?

(More laughter.)

BUFFY   I don't know, but I'm sure the corpse looks better!

(More laughter.)

FRED   *(Smiling)* All right...all right, let's move on to contestant #3, Jerry Mander...

(Everyone on stage freezes, panelists in midlaugh and contestants in their emotionally beaten-down state. An individual from off stage walks on, speaking conversationally and reading from a paper he or she is holding.)

WALK-ON SPEAKER   "Geek Search" was one of the most popular game shows of 1993 *(or insert current year)*. Since it is now 2013 *(or add 20 years to the current year)*, we thought you might want to know what has happened to our contestants.

Bud Tutwinkle changed his name and is currently head of neurological research at the Mayo Clinic. He is credited for making significant progress in the area of helping the paralyzed regain mobility.

Susan Slumppumper went on to college and earned a degree in fashion design. She currently makes more money in a year than the combined income of this city.

Jerry Mander, who we really didn't get a chance to hear from, didn't become a doctor or a millionaire. However, he is married with three great kids and a great wife. He loves his job and is very involved in his local church.

(This individual turns to exit, then turns back to the audience.)

Oh yes, as for Heather, Luke, and Buffy...no one knows where they are.

★★★

Discussion Starters

1. Did you find yourself laughing at the remarks made by the panelists? Have you ever found yourself in a real situation similar to this where someone is putting someone else down? How did you feel? What did you do?

2. Which, if any, of the characters did you most identify with? Why?

3. Write on a sheet of paper what you think you'll be doing in 20 years. Then pass in the papers to the leader. *(Randomly select an individual sheet of paper and read what's written on it. Then ask the group who they think wrote it and why. Carry this into a discussion of "other people's expectations of us.")*

The Good Old Days

---★---

Topic: *Pressure*

The Scene

A discussion between a parent and a teenager about the "good old days."

Characters

PARENT (mother or father)
TEENAGER (son or daughter)

★★★

(At home, a son or daughter is sitting, reading a textbook. A parent enters. This scene is not reliant on either character being male or female.)

PARENT	Dinner's ready.
TEENAGER	Okay. I'll be there in just a sec.
PARENT	*(Smiling)* Look at you. I'm envious.
TEENAGER	Huh?
PARENT	Seeing you study like that. It makes me wish I could be back in school again. *(Wistfully)* Ah, the good old days. Time to read, quizzes and tests, easy decisions...
TEENAGER	Ha! You can have them.
PARENT	You don't know what you're saying. I had to oversee three separate projects today, finish two major reports to the president of the company, and manage the directors of four departments. Some *major* decisions.

What did you do?

TEENAGER   *(Glibly)* Oh, nothing as important as that. I just spent the morning wrestling through midterm exams in math, science, and history that are worth half my final grade; trying to keep from throwing up when we ran track in gym; avoiding the drug dealers in the parking lot when I went to lunch; getting laughed at in the process because I don't even smoke cigarettes; fighting off the temptation to skip the rest of the day when (Scott/Pam)—(he's/she's) the best-looking babe in school—asked me to take a ride in (his/her) parent's new van; giving advice to Karen because Dave broke up with her before sixth period; having to do the same for Dave *after* sixth period; giving an oral report in English about the significance of Shakespeare's tragic heroes and making a fool of myself when I got Hamlet confused with Romeo; then getting pushed around by a gang of delinquents on my way home; and being traumatized to find out from an afternoon TV talk show that, statistically speaking, I'm the only virgin left in America. *(Pause.)* Are these *really* the good old days?

PARENT   *(A bewildered pause)* Dinner's ready.

TEENAGER   Thanks, I'll be right there.

(Parent exits. Teenager closes the book and does the same.)

Discussion Starters

1. Some parents refer to the "good old days"—times past when life seemed so much simpler. Do you think the times you now live in will become your "good old days"? Why or why not?

2. Do you think your parents understand the complexity of your life? Why or why not? Are your parents a good source of help and encouragement when you need someone to talk to? Why or why not?

3. Make a list of the most persistent, negative pressures in your life. Now make a list of the most persistent, positive influences in your life. Which list is longer? Which list has more power? From your list of pressures, discuss how you handle and control each one.

Hard Habit to Break

Topic: *Love*

The Scene

Two friends discuss a broken relationship.

Characters

JOE
TYRONE
DONNA

(This could take place anywhere. We enter in the middle of a scene in which Donna is standing, glaring furiously at Tyrone. She's obviously mad at him. Tyrone watches her wearily. Joe is uncomfortable.)

DONNA   All right, *don't* go with me. Stay here if you want!

(Donna storms off stage. Tyrone relaxes and sighs.)

JOE   *(Watching Tyrone curiously)* Aren't you gonna go after her?

TYRONE   *(Shaking his head)* I *always* go after her. She'll just have to get over it.

JOE   Yeah, but she was really mad.

TYRONE   I know it. But...you're my best friend. I oughta be able to stay here and talk to you if that's what I want to do. It's like she doesn't want me to talk to anybody...but her.

JOE   *(Shrugging)* That's how some girlfriends are.

TYRONE   But it's getting to be too much, you know? I'm really beginning to feel...you know, *trapped.*

JOE   I can't believe you're talking like this. Man, you guys have been together all the way through high school.

TYRONE I know. But you don't know what it's like. She depends on me. I mean, you just saw how it is—she wants us to be together *all the time.*

JOE   But...that's what girlfriends want when you, you know, love each other.

TYRONE *(Somberly)* Yeah, "love." That's what I keep thinking, too. But it's...suffocating. I can't get away. If I want a night out to hang around with you, she complains. If I say *she* should go out with friends, she says I'm trying to get rid of her. She won't let go of me.

JOE   Wow.

TYRONE I feel like I have to be everything for her. I'm her dad, her boyfriend, her teacher, her counselor...do you know what that's like? Sometimes I think I'm going crazy. Sometimes I think we're not boyfriend and girlfriend—we're some kind of bad habit.

JOE   *(Thoughtfully)* Hmm. That's strange.

TYRONE Yeah.*(Pauses, looks in the direction Donna exited, then to Joe.)* Do you really think I should go after her?

(They freeze.)

Discussion Starters

1. The Bible speaks of different kinds of love—love of God, sexual love, and love between friends. Describe each kind based on the following Bible verses: 1 Corinthians 13; 1 Samuel 18:1; 1 John 2:10; John 3:16; Ephesians 5:22-33; and 2 Samuel 13:1-15.

2. Would you say Tyrone's relationship with Donna was healthy? Why or why not? Do you believe they were really in love? Why or why not? What should be the attributes of a God-given and healthy love between two people—regardless of the type of relationship they have? List the characteristics of an "unhealthy" love (in your opinion).

3. Answer Tyrone's question for Joe. Should he go after her? Why or why not?

Helpless

------ ☆ ------

Topic: *Expectations*

The Scene

A mother reprimands her daughter for not doing her chores correctly.

Characters

MOTHER
CONNIE

★★★

(Mother is sitting at home when Connie walks through, headed for her room.)

CONNIE   Hi, Mom. I'll be in my room.

MOTHER   *(Stern tone, standing)* Wait just a minute, Connie. I want to talk to you.

CONNIE   *(Defensively)* What's wrong?

MOTHER   You're really helpless, aren't you?

CONNIE   What do you mean?

MOTHER   Fold the clothes from the dryer and put them away—that's a fairly easy thing to do.

CONNIE   I did.

MOTHER   Oh, really? You call that folding? Maybe I should give you a few refresher lessons. And you put the spare towels in the bathroom closet. You should know they belong in the *hall* closet.

CONNIE   I'm sorry.

MOTHER   Right. All you had to do was look and you would've seen. And your father would've had a fit if he'd seen how you put his shirts away.

CONNIE I said I was sorry.

MOTHER And I suppose you're going to tell me you vacuumed the stairs, too?

CONNIE Yeah, I did.

MOTHER Of course you did. That explains why the corners were *filthy* with lint. The vacuum cleaner comes with attachments for that, you know.

CONNIE I used the attachments. I didn't see any lint in the corners.

MOTHER Just like you didn't see the proper place for the spare towels. Or the right drawers for your dad's shirts.

CONNIE *(Upset)* I did the best I could! Why isn't it ever good enough for you?

MOTHER It's good enough when it's done *right*.

CONNIE But it's never done right unless *you* do it! I'm not you, all right? I'm not you!

(She storms off.)

MOTHER *(To herself)* Helpless. Completely helpless.

(She exits the opposite direction.)

Discussion Starters

1. Was Connie right? Was Connie's mother right? Were *both* right? Defend your answer.

2. Who did you sympathize with in the sketch? Explain. Have you ever been in a situation when you felt you couldn't please your parents no matter what you did? Give details and the outcome.

3. Put yourself in your parents' position for a moment. How can you (as a parent) push your child to do the best job possible without seeming like an unpleasant nag?

4. How should Connie and her mother resolve this conflict?

5. The Apostle Paul gives a word of instruction to fathers in Ephesians 6:4. How would you apply this verse to practical living?

If You Love Me...

Topic: *Love*

The Scene

An expectation about love becomes the central issue in an argument between a boyfriend and girlfriend.

Characters

LISA
MARK

★★★

(Mark and Lisa are at a table in the library.)

LISA   *(Concerned)* Mark?...Mark, are you mad at me?

MARK   *(Trying to study)* Hmm.

LISA   You better not be mad at me. *(Pausing, upset)* Mark, how could you even think about studying now? *(Pause.)* Mark? Mark!

MARK   *(With strained patience)* Lisa—I have a test.

LISA   Don't you think this is just a little more important than a stupid test?

MARK   No. We spent our whole lunch time yelling at each other about...about whatever it was we were yelling about. And we didn't get anything settled. And now I need to study.

LISA   *(Pause.)* I don't believe you. I thought you loved me.

MARK   *(Exasperated)* Lisa! *(Pause. Calmer but forcefully)* I do love you, but I have to pass this test!

LISA   I mean...I feel like our whole relationship is going down the tubes and...and you want to study. How could you want to study? Don't you love me? *(Pause.)* Mark? Mark!

MARK   *(Growling, getting up)* Forget it. I'll study somewhere else.

LISA   Oh, fine! Walk away! That's a good way to prove your love!

MARK   I'll see you after school!

(He exits.)

LISA   Maybe! I might have other plans...with someone who really loves me. *(Mumbling)* Jerk. *(Pause. Calling out)* Mark? *(She follows.)* Mark, wait. Did you hear me? Mark!

(She exits.)

Discussion Starters

1. "If you love me..." If anyone has ever used that phrase in your own experience, how did he or she finish the line? How did you respond? Have you ever used that phrase? Why did you use it and what did you require? What was the response? What are some other ways this phrase is used?

2. Is it ever right for a person to make demands of another person in the name of love? Why or why not? How might demands made in the name of love also be considered emotional blackmail? Can you think of any situations where this might be true? Describe them.

3. Read John 14:23 and John 15:10. What is the difference between the condition of love Jesus presents here and the way we place conditions on love?

Influence

---★---

Topic: *Media*

The Scene

Conflict arises over what influence the media has in our lives.

Characters

LAURIE

JIM

★★★

(Laurie and Jim are looking through the newspaper trying to choose a film to go to.)

LAURIE   This one looks pretty good.

JIM   "Lovesick"? *(Pause.)* Hey, I love the description here: "When passion collides with reality you become . . . Lovesick."

LAURIE   So?

JIM   Laurie, this is weak. It's just some cheap flick with a lot of grabbing and groping.

LAURIE   *(Playfully, smiling)* Yeah, so?

JIM   *(Only mildly amused)* Come on, Laurie. This is junk, and you know it.

LAURIE   Junk? Okay, so it's not "Decapitator 3." At least at the end of *this* movie they still have all their body parts.

JIM   Hey, I'm not going to those kind of films anymore.

LAURIE   Since when?

JIM   Since we started talking at youth group about the influence that films, music, and commercials have on us.

LAURIE   Are you serious?

JIM   Yeah.

LAURIE   Jim, films are just films. They're *fantasy*. What we're talking about at youth group has to do with people who are twisted—people who can't tell the difference between fantasy and reality—so they end up chopping up people with a meat cleaver and storing them in their freezer. No one gets chopped up in "Lovesick."

JIM   I know, but that's not the point. *(Pausing, thinking)* What kind of jeans do you have on?

LAURIE   Kelvin Kane, why?

JIM   Why didn't you buy some other brand?

LAURIE   Because I like these, and everyone else is wearing them.

JIM   And "everyone else" is wearing them because Julia Roberts *(or current "sex symbol")* wore them in her last film. They looked like they were painted on.

LAURIE   It sounds like *you're* being a little "influenced," too!

JIM   I *am*. The reason I wanted these athletic shoes was because all the commercials I saw made me think that they'd help me dunk a basketball. And if that didn't work, they'd at least help me pick up some babes. *(Jokingly)* I figure that's the real reason you even go out with me.

LAURIE   *(Smiling)* No. Actually, it's because you wear that Old Spike cologne, *(dramatically)* "...the scent that unleashes the beast in every woman."

JIM   See! That's my point. You even know their ad line.

LAURIE   So? *(Holding up a can of soft drink)* I know the theme song for this soft drink, too, but that doesn't *make* me go out and buy it.

JIM   I know it didn't *make* you buy it. But it *did* influence your decision. That's all I'm saying.

LAURIE   So? Big deal. We're only talking soft drinks and jeans, for heaven's sake, not mass murder!

JIM   Right, but if a little 30-second commercial can "influence" what we wear or what we drink, how much more can a three-minute song or two-hour movie affect how we think and act?

LAURIE *(Pausing, then standing to exit)* Jim?

JIM Yeah?

LAURIE You're worse than my parents. *I'm* going to the movie.

(She exits.)

JIM Laurie!

(He exits, following her.)

Discussion Starters

1. List some of your favorite films, songs, and commercials. Why do you like them? What most attracts you to a new movie or a song? Explain.

2. Can you identify any way in which the media have influenced your thinking or your actions?

3. Read Philippians 4:8. How should this Scripture affect our thinking? What are some practical ways to apply this Scripture to our lives?

Nagging

Topic: *Nagging*

The Scene

A father berates his son for not getting the lawn mower fixed.

Characters

FATHER

ANDY

★★★

(In his garage, Andy is kneeling over a lawn mower, poking at it with a screwdriver. Father stands above him.)

FATHER *(Growling to himself)* I said this would happen. Didn't I say this would happen? Well, Andrew?

ANDY Looks like this lawn mower has given up the ghost. I think it's the carburetor.

FATHER This wouldn't be the same carburetor that I told you last month to have fixed?

ANDY They only have one—so I guess it is. *(Sighing as he stands up)* I'll call the shop.

FATHER *(Angrily)* The shop won't do us much good now. How could you let this happen? Week after week I told you to get it into the shop. The yard looks like a jungle as it is. Why can't you be more responsible?

ANDY I'm sorry. I thought it would last longer.

FATHER Uh-huh. And how many times did I tell you?

ANDY Over and over, Dad.

FATHER But you don't listen to me, do you? Why don't you ever listen to me? It's not as if I nag you about incidentals.

ANDY   No, Dad. Only the important things.

FATHER   I warned you this would happen. Didn't I warn you? I swear, Andy, I don't understand why you never listen to me.

(Father exits angrily. Andy looks at the audience, sighs, then follows Father out.)

Discussion Starters

1. The father in this sketch claims that he doesn't understand why his son never listens to him. What would you tell the father in response? Explain.

2. Define "nagging." Would you say this father was a nag? Is nagging someone a good method for getting them to do something? Why or why not? Why do you suppose so many people in authority nag those under them?

3. Do you ever nag? Who and why? Do they respond by doing what you've nagged them to do? If not, what do you do next? How do you respond when someone nags you?

4. Rather than nagging, what's a better way of asking someone to do something?

The "Oughta-Be" Club

Topic: *Parents*

The Scene

Five teenagers discuss their frustration with their parents' expectations.

Characters

MIKE   **JIM**
JASON   **BRET**
SHERI

(In a meeting room. Four high school guys and a girl enter and sit in a semicircle, all looking a bit uncomfortable.)

MIKE   Okay...well, welcome to our first meeting of the "Oughta-Be" club. I'm Mike Williams, and I'm glad you're here. *(Pauses as the other four give him a look as if to say, "What in the world are you doing?" Then smiles, trying to be overly friendly.)* Why don't we begin by telling a little bit about ourselves. Like, what do you like about school or what's your favorite fast food.

(The others are completely silent as they stare either at Mike or at the floor.)

MIKE   *(Trying to cover for the deafening silence)* Okay...well, how 'bout where you've traveled in your life or famous people you've met?

(Complete silence.)

MIKE   Or perhaps you've got a good fishing story that...

JASON *(Cutting him off)* Knock it off, Mike...What d'ya think this is, Mr. Nurdlinger's psychology class?

BRET Yeah, I thought this was going to be a club, not a therapy group.

JASON So, what're we gonna do? Four guys and a girl don't exactly make a club.

MIKE Look, you know why we're all here. I figured that if we got together, we could compare notes and find a way to get our parents off our backs. Okay?

JIM *(Sheepishly)* I'll start.

MIKE Go for it.

JIM Well, my parents keep telling me I "oughta be" deciding *right now* what I'm going to be doing in 20 years. I have a *hard enough* time thinking about what I'm going to do *tomorrow*.

BRET Hey, don't complain. At least you *have* a mom and a dad. My mom is so worried about me becoming a loser like my dad, she doesn't trust me. And she's constantly comparing me to my older brother: "You oughta be like Dennis...he'd *never* do this or that!" She's convinced that if she stays on my case enough, I'll turn out to be the perfect son. All I want to do is be *me*.

SHERI Your mom doesn't sound so bad. Maybe she's a little over-protective, but she *cares*. My folks let me do anything I want. I mean *sometimes* they kinda suggest that I "oughta be" doing this or I "oughta be" thinking about that...but they never follow through. I could tell them that I've chosen to become a mass murderer and they'd say, "Oh, that's wonderful, honey...whatever makes you happy." I just want someone to *help me* choose what to do and where to go.

JASON Hey, *I* don't have any choices. My parents have already made up my mind for me. I can hear my dad giving me the "when you go to college, you 'oughta be' the starting quarterback...you 'oughta be' the best student at the university...you 'oughta be' grateful for all we've given you." The fact is, all his oughta-bes are what he never "got to be." He's forcing me to live out all of *his* dreams.

(Awkward silence.)

MIKE   So, we all know what we oughta be...but what are we "gonna be"?

(They all look at one another despondently and shrug their shoulders.)

Discussion Starters

1. Do you feel a lot of "oughta-be" pressure on you? Explain. Who does it come from? How do you react to it? What are some of the things you're told you oughta be?

2. Are there any oughta-bes that are good? If so, identify them and tell why they are good. If you could offer our skit characters any advice about their parents, what would you say?

Person on the Street

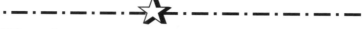

Topic: *Church attendance*

The Scene

People are stopped on the street and asked why they attend church.

Characters

HOST
EIGHT PEOPLE (of varying ages as indicated in the script)

(An interviewer—the Host—can be located either on or off stage. People enter alternately from one side of the stage or the other.)

HOST   Welcome to another edition of "Man on the Street," or to be more politically correct, "PERSON on the Street." I'm standing outside of *(name of your city or town)* Community Church after the Sunday-morning service asking people why they attend church. And here comes a couple of sharp-looking individuals. *(Two guys cross the stage.)* Excuse me!

GUYS   *(Expressionless)* Yeah?

HOST   We're doing a brief survey and were wondering if you would mind telling our listening audience why you attend church?

GUYS   *(Pointing to each other)* Because *he* does.

(They exit.)

HOST	Insightful. Ah, here comes another young person. Excuse me, why do *you* attend church?
TEEN	Attend church? Forget it! Church is boring, stupid, and a place where old ladies and jerks hang out. I was just passing by on my way to the arcade.
HOST	I see. Have you ever *been* to church before?
TEEN	Are you kidding? Why would I want to hang out with a bunch of old ladies and hypocrites?

(Teen exits.)

HOST	Articulate. Well, let's try this young lady. Excuse me, miss, why do *you* attend church?
GIRL	Because my parents make me.
HOST	I see. Well, is there any *other* reason why you attend?
GIRL	Sure . . . there's a couple of cute guys whose parents make *them* attend, too.

(She exits.)

HOST	Hmm. And here's an older gentleman . . . Sir, could you tell me *why* you attend church?
MAN	Why do I attend church? Well, I was raised in this denomination and feel a certain sense of obligation to attend.
HOST	Well, do you find "meaning" in the services?
MAN	Oh sure! As long as the minister *(or pastor)* doesn't go past noon, I enjoy the sermons well enough. Except when he harps on money. I can't stand too much money talk. *(He exits.)*
HOST	Indeed. Ah, here's a lovely young couple. Pardon me, could you tell me *why* you attend church?
WIFE	*(Looking lovingly at her husband)* Well, our son just turned 5, and we felt it was important that he begin receiving some religious training.
HUSBAND	*(Looking lovingly at his wife)* Yeah, we don't normally go to church, but we thought this might help him when he grows up . . . you know, to be a better person.

(Husband and wife exit.)

HOST   Compelling. Well, let's try one last person. Excuse me, could you tell me why you attend church?

MAN   *(Quietly, unassumingly)* Uh, I don't go to church.

HOST   Not again...

MAN   Oh, it's not that I don't want to...in fact, I *do* want to attend. It's just that no one has ever invited me.

HOST   Why don't you just walk in?

MAN   I just couldn't. I wouldn't feel comfortable, and I don't want to impose.

(He exits.)

HOST   *(Thoughtfully)* Hmm. Well, there you have it—a clear and compelling view of the church. We've asked a cross section of people why they attend church, but we have one more person to ask. *(To audience)* Why do *you* attend church?

★★★

Discussion Starters

1. Encourage everyone to answer the Host's question, "Why do you attend church?" Discuss both the positive and negative answers given.

2. Do you think Jesus would feel at home in our church? Why or why not? Do you think Jesus would feel "forgotten" in our church? Why or why not? Do you think Jesus feels forgotten by you sometimes? Explain. Do you include Jesus in your church experience? Why or why not? If you do, how do you do it?

3. If you were to start your own church, what would you do differently from what you experience in your own church? Have you ever tried to incorporate any of these ideas in your youth group? What was the response?

The Pest

Topic: *Unwanted love*

The Scene

A young woman wants to get rid of an unwanted suitor.

Characters

SUE
DEBBIE

★★★

(In the school cafeteria, Sue and Debbie are sitting, eating. Suddenly, something in the distance catches Sue's eye.)

SUE   Debbie! Look who just came in. It's Tom.

DEBBIE   Oh no. *(Trying to hide)* I hope he doesn't see me.

SUE   What? You're kidding, right?

DEBBIE   No, I'm serious. If he comes over here, I'm leaving.

SUE   But it's *Tom*! I thought... you know.

DEBBIE   I don't want him to see me. He's driving me nuts.

SUE   All right, all right. Relax. He's gone.

DEBBIE   *(Relieved)* Good.

SUE   So—what's going on?

DEBBIE   Nothing. I just don't want to see him, that's all.

SUE   I don't get you. I thought you guys were friends. Isn't he the one who's been putting those cute notes in your locker and all that?

DEBBIE   Yeah, that's the problem. I thought we were friends, and... he started getting weird. You know, serious.

SUE	So?
DEBBIE	So, I don't like him in that way.
SUE	Oh. *(Pause.)* Did you tell him?
DEBBIE	Yeah, and he still won't leave me alone. It's getting to be a pain.
SUE	But he's so cute.
DEBBIE	He's driving me crazy. He keeps showing up after my classes and wants to take me home from school, and...and I think he keeps calling my house and hanging up.
SUE	That's creepy.
DEBBIE	Yeah. I wanted to be nice to him—but now he's really bugging me. I don't know how to make him go away. I wish we could just be friends again...

(They freeze.)

Discussion Starters

1. Have you ever been in a situation like this? Explain. How did you handle it? Debbie confesses that she doesn't know how to make Tom go away. What would you suggest?

2. Put yourself in Tom's position: He obviously likes Debbie a lot and isn't taking the hint that she won't return his affection. What should he do? What would you do if you were him?

3. Some people believe an "unrequited love" can be overcome through persistence and determination. Do you believe that's true? Why or why not?

4. Let's change the sketch for a moment. Tom not only cares a great deal for Debbie (beyond friendship), but he has also prayed about it and believes that it's God's will for them to be together. Side with Debbie and respond. Side with Tom and respond. How can you determine God's will in who you choose to date—and even marry?

A Quality Education

Topic: *Education*

The Scene

One friend finds out the *real* reason the other is excited about going back to school.

Characters

ROBIN   **NICK**
MELANIE

(Robin and Melanie are standing in the aisle of a local drugstore or stationery shop. Robin is elated about what she sees.)

ROBIN   *(Smiling)* Am I in heaven or is it my imagination?

MELANIE   Heaven? The day before school starts, and you think it's heaven?

ROBIN   *(Genuinely excited)* Look around you, Mel—stacks of new notebooks, unused yellow pads, pencils waiting to be sharpened . . . it's enough to make a girl cry.

MELANIE   Or gag. *(Pause.)* Let me guess . . . either your dad's bribing you again to get A's or you've developed a warped desire to hang out in the stationery aisle at Walgreens.

ROBIN   Neither. I've simply grown in my understanding of the importance of a quality education and its eventual application to my adult life.

MELANIE   *(Pausing, staring)* Malaria.

ROBIN	Pardon?
MELANIE	Malaria. Repeated infection from mosquitoes eventually causing brain rot. You've been assaulted by a swarm.
ROBIN	Very funny. One day you'll look back on this moment and wish that you'd paused long enough to consider your personal future.
MELANIE	One day *you'll* look back on this moment and plead "temporary insanity."
ROBIN	Yeah, right. Think of it this way, Mel. Our summer of frivolous activity is over, and new adventures in learning lay in wait around every hallway and locker.

(Nick enters.)

NICK	Hi, Robin. Hey, I'm glad I ran into you at registration the other day. Helping you with your geometry should be a kick. See you tomorrow.

(Robin lights up, clearly exposing her <u>real</u> desire for "education.")

MELANIE	"New adventures in learning," huh? And exactly which locker will he be "laying in wait" around?

(They freeze.)

Discussion Starters

1. Do you like school? Why or why not? Choose a word to describe what you feel the day before you go back to school after summer vacation. Is it different from what you feel when returning from Christmas vacation? Why or why not?

2. What's most important to you about school? least important? What are some personal goals you have for this school year? What's one new goal you could add to that list?

Questions About Len

Topic: *Suicide*

The Scene

An unidentified speaker tells us about a guy who killed himself.

Character

SPEAKER (the speaker could be either male or female)

(Speaker enters, then addresses the audience.)

SPEAKER   Len killed himself last Saturday. He got ahold of his dad's gun and...did it. I didn't know him very well. At least, not since we were in elementary school together. We hung around different groups when we got into junior high. He started doing a lot of sports, and I didn't. He was good. Captain of this, coach of that. He was the all-star. In high school, he played everything—he was everybody's favorite. He was president of the student council our sophomore year and again this year. So, the whole school is shocked. The teachers are comparing notes. The kids talk about it in the cafeteria. "How could somebody like Len kill himself?" they ask. "He had looks, talent, ability, popularity...everything you'd want. Everything to *live* for. And he killed himself. How could somebody like Len do that?" That's what everyone's asking. *(Pause.)*

Funny. I wonder if everyone would ask the same questions about somebody like *me*?

(Speaker exits.)

★★★

Discussion Starters

1. The picture we get of Len is that he had everything to live for—based on his looks, talent, ability, popularity, and status. Is this "list" a good way to gauge someone's success in life? Why or why not? In your opinion, what is worth living for?

2. Why do you think people kill themselves? What do you think is worth killing yourself over? Has anyone you've known committed suicide? What was the public reaction? What was your own personal reaction? Have you ever thought about suicide? If so, why? Do you think about it now? (If you do, we would encourage you to speak with your group leader as soon as this session is ended.)

Note: Group leaders should be prepared for a variety of reactions to this topic—especially if any of the group members confess to having thought about suicide. If you are not equipped to counsel potential suicides (and don't assume you are), get the number of local Christian telephone hot lines to hand out or, better still, have a trained counselor present for this discussion. The authors highly recommend the book *Why Suicide?* by Jerry Johnston (Nelson Publishing) for group leaders and members in preparation for this meeting.

Russian Roulette

Topic: *Premarital sex*

The Scene

A teenage girl tries to decide whether maintaining her virginity is important.

Characters

SANDY
JENNIFER
HEATHER

★★★

(Three girls, Heather, Sandy, and Jennifer, are sitting in a semicircle all with very serious, intense, and concerned appearances. Jennifer has a gun in her lap that she occasionally picks up and examines thoughtfully.)

SANDY	So you're really going to go ahead with this?
JENNIFER	*(As if she's been asked this same question many times before)* Yes!
HEATHER	But, Jen, we love you. Your parents love you.
JENNIFER	Yeah . . . so?
SANDY	Yeah . . . so?! Jennifer, this is your *life* we're talking about here . . . not taking a trip to the 7-Eleven!
JENNIFER	That's the point . . . it's *my* life, not *yours.*
HEATHER	Oh, I get it. I'm supposed to just sit back and let you . . .
JENNIFER	*(Cutting her off, resolved)* I know that this is the right thing to do.
HEATHER	You're confused. That's all.

JENNIFER	I've never been more sure. *(Pause.)* I've been dumped by my last two boyfriends, and I'm not going to let it happen again. I can't take the embarrassment or the hurt.
SANDY	But this is crazy! Look, give it a few more days... you'll change your mind.
JENNIFER	No. Tonight's the night. *(She stands to go.)*
HEATHER	Where are you going? *(Pausing, no answer)* Jennifer!
SANDY	Jenny, come on... please?
HEATHER AND SANDY	*(Having paused with no response from Jennifer)* Where?!
JENNIFER	*Mike's* house, all right?! His mom's out of town, and his dad works late. It's the perfect place.
HEATHER	Jennifer, this is... *suicide.*
JENNIFER	You're *so* dramatic. Hey, it's only *sex.* What do you think I'm going to do? *(Lifting the gun, smiling)* Use my brother's water gun and "end it all"?
SANDY	Jennifer, it's not funny. You're not only giving up something you can only give away once, you're doing something you know is wrong... *and* dangerous.

(Jennifer begins to exit as Sandy and Heather follow.)

JENNIFER	Don't start preaching at me.
HEATHER AND SANDY	*(Pleading)* Jennifer...

(They freeze.)

Discussion Starters

1. Do you feel pressure at your school to be sexually active? Why or why not? Discuss ways you can help each other remain sexually pure.

2. Which is emphasized more in your school—abstinence or "safe sex"? Which do you think is the best approach? Explain. What "dangers" are you afraid of when it comes to having sex before you're married? Why?

Sisters

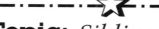

Topic: *Sibling rivalry*

The Scene

Two sisters argue constantly yet wonder why their mother reacts the way she does.

Characters

SAGE
ERIN
MOTHER

★★★

(Erin is standing in Sage's closet rummaging through her clothes.)

SAGE   *(Upset)* Get out of my closet!

ERIN   I'm just borrowing a blouse.

SAGE   *Just* borrowing? The last time you "just borrowed" something it took three weeks to find it!

ERIN   That's because Julie needed it for Mitch's party, but her sister Angie loaned it to Lisa because she thought it was Julie's and didn't know that she had borrowed it, then Lisa loaned it to Michelle who wore it once and pitted it out, so Michelle took it to the cleaners and forgot it was there until her mom picked it up and asked whose it was and why she had to pay for it to be cleaned. She's kinda ticked so you might want to call her and apologize.

SAGE   What I "might want to" do is stuff you down the garbage disposal...now get out of my closet.

ERIN   Hey, you borrow stuff from me all the time.

SAGE   Baloney. When was the last time?

ERIN	Yesterday when you borrowed my belt.
SAGE	That doesn't count...it's an old belt.
ERIN	All right, then how 'bout last week when you borrowed my new jeans?
SAGE	Those jeans didn't cost half as much as my blouse.
ERIN	So? What does that have to do with anything?
SAGE	*Everything.* If I lost your jeans, which I didn't, it wouldn't have cost hardly anything to replace them, and within the scope of who's borrowed what and how many times, there's no competition...you are the Mooch Queen. Now, get out of my closet. *(Pause.)* Hey, have you seen my green, bulky-knit sweater?
ERIN	You mean the one you *borrowed* from *me?*
SAGE	No way! It's mine.
ERIN	Wrong! Mom and Dad gave it to me last Christmas. It's just that you've borrowed it so much, you started thinking it was *yours.*
SAGE	*(Hesitantly realizing)* Oh, yeah...well, where is it? It's my favorite, and I want to wear it tonight.
ERIN	*(Smiling impishly)* Surely you jest! Why should the "Mooch Queen" choose to be so kind?
SAGE	Because if the "Mooch Queen" doesn't, I'm going to pound "her highness" into the pavement.
ERIN	*(Getting a bit louder)* Oooo! Another threat!
SAGE	*(Louder still)* Knock it off and let me have the sweater!
ERIN	*(Adamantly)* No way!!
SAGE	*(Angrily)* Listen, you selfish little twerp, tell me where that sweater is!
ERIN	*(Equally angry and defiant)* Over my dead body!
SAGE	All right, have it your way!

(With a threatening move, Sage lunges at Erin as if to begin chasing her. Just as she does, their mother enters, and they run right into her.)

MOTHER   *(Upset)* What in the world is going on in here?!

SAGE   *(Simultaneously with Erin, loudly)* Erin is being a real jerk and won't let me borrow her sweater that she never wears even though she knows how much I really like it, but does she care? No!

ERIN   *(Simultaneously with Sage, loudly)* Sage thinks she owns the world and is always trying to boss me around, and all I was doing was looking through her stuff to see if there was anything I could wear...

MOTHER   *(Angrily cutting them off)* Stop it!! I'm tired of you two constantly arguing and calling each other names! Now, Erin, get out of Sage's closet, and, Sage, quit threatening your sister. If I hear one more peep out of either of you, I'm putting you both on restriction!

(She exits in a huff.)

(Both girls are caught in a frozen stare as she exits. After a couple of seconds they both look at each other with a rather quizzical expression.)

ERIN   What's *her* problem?

SAGE   She's a parent; she's supposed to be that way. *(Pause.)* Now, can I borrow that sweater?

ERIN   Sure. *(Pause.)* Parents...they always overreact.

(They exit.)

Discussion Starters

1. How many brothers and sisters do you have? What are their names and ages? What part of this skit sounds familiar in your family?

2. When there is conflict between you and your siblings, do you think that your parents tend to
  ● be overreactive,
  ● not get involved,
  ● take sides, or
  ● threaten, but not follow through.
What do you think their reaction should be?

3. Read Genesis 4:1-12. How was the conflict between Cain and Abel like the conflicts you have with your siblings? What is the biggest area of conflict between you and your siblings? Why?

Slime Time TV

_—_ _—_ _·_ _—_ _·_ _—_ _·_ ★ _—_ _·_ _—_ _·_ _—_ _·_ _—_ _·_ _—_

Topic: _Television_

The Scene

Two teenagers discuss the merits of television programs.

Characters

LISA
BRIAN

★★★

(Brian and Lisa are talking after watching Lisa's favorite TV show.)

LISA   I love that show.

BRIAN   It's all right.

LISA   All right? Brian, this show is a classic. It's one of the few TV programs that shows high school kids like they really are.

BRIAN   Yeah, I really identify with those guys. Perfect looks, unlimited bank accounts, great friends, and unbelievable problems that can always be solved in an hour. I need to invite them over to _my_ house.

LISA   Okay, so they aren't exactly like you and me, but it's something we can always hope for.

BRIAN   Hope for?! You _hope_ to get pregnant, have an abortion, _and_ suffer from a debilitating learning disorder, only to discover later that you have an inoperable brain tumor?

LISA   _(Curtly)_ No, I was thinking more along the lines of the "unlimited bank accounts."

BRIAN   Face it, Lisa, you're addicted to fantasy television.

LISA   Don't talk to _me_ about "fantasy" on television. You spend most of your time glued to the tube watching a bunch of gorillas, growling, grabbing, and sweating on each other.

BRIAN *(Indignantly)* Hey, professional wrestling is a tough sport!

LISA Right, and "Playboy" is an anatomy magazine.

BRIAN I don't think there's any comparison between "Palm Springs, 90219" and Pro Wrestling.

LISA *(Sarcastically)* Now *there's* something we can agree upon. *(Pause.) You're* the one who's addicted.

BRIAN I can take it or leave it.

LISA Sure you can.

BRIAN I can! I'll make you a deal. I'll quit watching my show if you'll stop watching yours.

LISA *(Shaking his hand)* Deal! *(Pausing, thinking)* But how are we gonna know if the other's cheating?

BRIAN We'll each tell our younger sister about the deal. They'd squeal on us in a heartbeat.

LISA Gotcha. This will be good for us. *(Pausing)* So...what are you gonna do during that hour?

BRIAN I don't know. Maybe I'll catch "All-Star Gladiators." How 'bout you?

LISA "Love Lives of the Rich and Famous"!

(They exit.)

Discussion Starters

1. How many hours a day do you think you watch TV?

2. What are some of your favorite shows? Why? What's the thing you like most about television? What do you like least about it? Do you think television's effect on our society has been overall positive or negative? Explain. What about television's effect on your own life—has it been positive or negative? Explain.

3. If you were to give up one hour a day of TV viewing, what would you do with that time? Read Ephesians 4:17-32. What would qualify as a "wise" use of your time?

The Talk

---★---

Topic: *Expressing true feelings*

The Scene

A young man thinks about having a heart-to-heart talk with his dad.

Characters

DOUG
FATHER

★★★

(Doug's bedroom. The trick with this sketch is that Doug should address the audience as if he's talking to his dad.)

DOUG *(With nervous determination)* Dad, I think it's time we had a talk. *(Puts up a hand)* No, now don't say anything until I've finished. You always get to speak your mind, and now it's my turn. I've been your son for a long time—since birth, I guess—and I've tried to be a good son. You know—gone along with what you wanted. Even when I didn't really *want* to, I did it because I thought it would make you happy. Maybe I was wrong. You decided my life, Dad. Every detail. And sometimes that was good, but other times...I wish you would've asked me, Dad. Just once. I wish you would've asked me what *I* thought. Let me talk about *my* feelings. Just once. But you didn't. And I'm fed up, Dad. The rules are going to change around here. I'm going to be my own person...my own man.

(Father calls from off stage, startling Doug.)

FATHER Doug?

DOUG Huh? What?

FATHER Supper's ready. Come on.

DOUG   Right, Dad. In a jiff.

FATHER   *(Entering, looking around)* Are you alone? I thought I heard you saying something?

DOUG   No, Dad. It's just me—talking to myself.

FATHER   Oh. Well, hurry up.

(Father exits.)

DOUG   *(Calling out to his dad in a weak voice)* Dad?

FATHER   *(Poking his head back into Doug's room)* Yes, Doug?

DOUG   *(Nervously, acting as if he's going to tell his dad how he feels)* Um . . . well . . . I was wondering . . . *(Pause. Then with resignation)* What's for supper?

(Both exit.)

Discussion Starters

1. Have you ever felt like Doug? Explain. Have you ever told your parents anything like the things Doug wants to say to his father? Be specific about what you would say to them if you could.

2. If Doug actually said these things to his father, how do you think his father would react? How would *your* father or mother react if you said to either of them the things you wish you could say? Why do you think they'd react that way?

3. Play counselor for a moment. How would you advise Doug and his father if they came to you for help? What would you ask Doug to do? What would you ask his father to do?

4. Do you ever have times when you wish you could get out from under your parents' authority? If so, when do you feel it most keenly? What do you do about those feelings? Do you talk to your parents about those feelings? Why or why not?

Tolerance

---★---

Topic: *Tolerance*

The Scene

A group of teenagers involved in student government discuss the importance of being tolerant of everyone's views—except those they disagree with.

Characters

STEVE   JUDY
BILL   SUE
DAVE   MARK

★★★

(Six teenagers are seated in a semicircle facing the audience. Steve is seated in the center, Judy is to his immediate right, and Bill is to Judy's right. Dave is seated to the immediate left of Steve with Sue next to him and Mark on the end. These are people who are very conscious of looking the part of the thoughtful, concerned student. Mark does not draw attention to himself, but he is clearly not a part of this group.)

STEVE   Well, let's begin this meeting of our student council. We have only a few things on our agenda to deal with to-day. *(Looking at a sheet of paper)* Let's see, we have to debate whether or not to recommend our cafeteria be shut down for health reasons...though I don't think that'll be much of a "debate." Also on the docket we have a special presentation by our head janitor, Mr. Toddlehopper, updating us on the new renovations to the guys' restrooms. And finally, we need to discuss a very serious problem that has arisen in our student body lately: intolerance. Judy and Dave, you brought this to our attention, so why don't you lead off. Judy?

JUDY   Well, as you know, Central High has always been known for its openness and acceptance of *all* people... their cultural and ethnic heritage and beliefs. We have demonstrated this by converting our football weight-room three months ago into the Multi-Ethnic Love of Humankind Eco-Diversity Cultural Center for the Socially Concerned. Both people who visited have expressed their support and gratitude.

BILL AND SUE   *(Agreeing)* Yes, it was very nice.

SUE   I especially appreciated the pictures showing the oppressed peoples of our country being trampled underfoot by degenerate tyrants like Christopher Columbus.

BILL   Hey, when you get right down to it, that guy's responsible for the mess this country's in today!

DAVE   Well, that, in part, is what we want to discuss today. We have made every effort to change all school policies that restrict or in any way discriminate against various people. Over the past two years we have made tremendous strides in promoting tolerance by such critical policies as allowing individuals to bring their pets to the prom. Abolishing what remained of the dress code and allowing students to wear anything that helps them express their true individualism. And we recently installed dispensers in the restrooms that help promote wise and safe use of our bodies.

JUDY   Gracefully put, Dave.

DAVE   Thanks.

JUDY   But a blight has raised its ugly head amongst us. That is the blight of intolerance. Some people at this school have even had the audacity to express opposition to some of these and other policies of openness we have established. In fact, one such person is actually *on* this student council and is sitting with us today! *(Everyone snaps their heads to the left, staring at Mark. Mark smiles.)* Mark, would you care to explain to this group *why* you have chosen to oppose most everything we have endorsed?

MARK   *(Thoughtfully, with warm disposition)* Well, I think it's important to note that I'm *not* opposed to everything. In fact, I was involved in helping set up the student 800 help line, and I still volunteer my time on the weekends. I also organized the food drive for the hungry and helped serve Thanksgiving dinner to the homeless.

JUDY   Yes, but isn't there some "religious" group behind those programs?

MARK   Well, yes . . . so?

DAVE   Sooo, there's more to feeding the hungry than just feeding the hungry.

MARK   What do you mean?

JUDY   Well, we all know that *those* groups have another "hidden" agenda . . . one that is very *intolerant* of other people's views.

MARK   If "intolerance" means that they actually take a stand for things they believe in and follow through with their actions, then I suppose they're guilty as charged. But I can tell you that the only thing they really are intolerant of is hypocrisy . . . talking about doing something to help others but never really doing it.

BILL   Could we move on to the cafeteria debate?

DAVE   (*Ignoring Bill's remark*) You narrow-minded right-wingers are all the same. Trying to get everybody to believe what *you* believe while doing your little "good deeds." Personally, I won't put up with it.

MARK   You mean, you won't "tolerate" it?

DAVE AND JUDY   (*They look at each other and then back at Mark*) Exactly.

MARK   Just checking.

STEVE   Well, it's apparent that a motion is in order. I move that Mark be removed from this student council and that only those with tolerant views be allowed to participate. All in favor? (*Everyone but Mark raises his or her hand.*) Passed. Now, Mark, if you'll excuse us, Mr. Toddlehopper is waiting to come in and make his important presentation. *(Calling out)* Fred, come on in!

(They freeze.)

Discussion Starters

1. Do you think your school's policies are tolerant of different groups? Is the school tolerant of Christians? Why or why not? Do you think the students are tolerant of different groups? What kinds of things won't they tolerate? What kinds of groups do you have trouble tolerating? Explain.

2. What does the Bible say about tolerance toward one another? God's tolerance toward us? What one word describes his tolerance? Do you think Jesus was tolerant of all the groups he was around when he walked the earth? Why or why not? Which group did he tolerate the least? (The religious leaders.) Why do you think he had such a hard time with this group?

Too Late

---★---

Topic: *Time management*

The Scene

A terminal latecomer discovers a consequence for his tardiness.

Characters

PETER
MOTHER

★★★

(At home, Mother is at a table drinking some tea. Peter peeks in as if he's dashing out for the evening.)

PETER   Okay, Mom, see you later.

MOTHER   Hold on. Don't rush off. Lance called while you were in the shower. They decided to go on without you.

PETER   They did *what?*! *(Angrily)* Those jerks! How could they go without me? Idiots!

MOTHER   It's your own fault, Peter. You were supposed to meet them 45 minutes ago. I'm surprised it doesn't happen more often considering how late you are for everything.

PETER   It's not my fault! I can't help it if I have things to do.

MOTHER   Like what?

PETER   You know, like, get ready and all that.

MOTHER   You were upstairs listening to your stereo. The bass was vibrating so much I think I lost a couple of fillings.

PETER   Well, I lost track of time.

MOTHER   Right. You *always* lose track of time. And people get tired of it. Being late all the time shows a complete lack of respect for other people. It's like you're saying, "Hey, my time is more important than yours." So it's up to you. If you want to keep your friends, you'll probably have to work on your time management. That's all.

PETER   *(Sarcastically)* Thanks, Mom. Glad you saw my side of it.

MOTHER   No sides to it, sweetheart. What are you going to do now?

PETER   Can I borrow the car?

MOTHER   Well . . . *(Looking at watch, jumping up)* Oops—no—I'm late picking up your father at the station!

(She scrambles off in a mad rush. Peter turns to the audience and shrugs his shoulders, then freezes.)

Discussion Starters

1. Respond to the mother's statement that being late shows a lack of respect for other people. Do you agree? Why or why not? Do you think "being free to do your own thing" is more important than keeping your promises to people? Why or why not?

2. Do you know someone who is always late for things? How do you feel when you're kept waiting for him or her? What reasons does this person often give for being late? Do you believe him or her? Why or why not? Are you late very often? What can you do to be a better manager of your time?

3. What does always being late tell others about your character? How might that negatively influence someone's view of Christianity?

Unequal

---★---

Topic: *Dating*

The Scene

A teenager confronts her friend about her choice in boyfriends.

Characters

LAURA

CARLA

★★★

(In a school cafeteria. Laura approaches Carla who is sitting, nibbling on a sandwich.)

LAURA Oh, *there* you are. I've been looking for you.

CARLA What's wrong? Did I miss something?

LAURA No, I was just wondering what happened to you yesterday.

CARLA Yesterday?

LAURA Church. Remember? Sunday-morning service? You and me— third pew back on the left?

CARLA I was...away.

LAURA Again.

CARLA What "again"?

LAURA That makes three Sundays in a row.

CARLA Did the church put you in charge of the attendance records?

LAURA Why don't you admit it? You were with Dan yesterday. And the reason you weren't in church the week before is because you were out late with Dan the night before. And the week before that, you...

CARLA   *(Interrupting)* All right. So, what's your point? You must've been talking to my mom. Dan is just a friend.

LAURA   "Just a friend"? I know you better than that. I hope you know what you're getting into.

CARLA   Laura, listen to me...there's nothing to worry about. He's a nice guy. He's a lot of fun.

LAURA   But he's not a Christian.

CARLA   But he knows *I* am. There's nothing to worry about, Laura. Trust me.

LAURA   *(Cautioning)* Carla...

CARLA   *(Defensively)* I like being with him, that's all. He's...different from the guys at church. He's not so stuffy and boring, and he doesn't spend all his time second-guessing whether he's allowed to have fun or not. And, unlike some Christians we know very well, he's a perfect gentleman.

LAURA   So?

CARLA   So...I like him. But I'll be careful. You just watch and see. I'll be very careful.

(They freeze.)

Discussion Starters

1. Should Christians ever date non-Christians? If so, under what conditions? If not, why not? What are the dangers in becoming intimately involved with someone who isn't a Christian? What are the advantages?

2. Read aloud 2 Corinthians 6:14-18. What does the Bible say about Christians who become intimately involved with someone who isn't a Christian?

3. What about Carla's assessment of her Christian dates being "stuffy and boring" and even "ungentlemanly"? Is that true, girls? And what about you guys—what do you think of the Christian girls you go out with? What are other solutions to this problem besides going out with non-Christians?

The Worst Offense

Topic: *Cheating*

The Scene

A guy talks to his friend about his dilemma.

Characters

BRAD
JASON

★★★

(Brad and Jason are talking. Brad is obviously upset.)

BRAD   I can't believe it. I just can't believe it!

JASON   Will you calm down!

BRAD   *(Not calmly)* I *am* calm! *(Reacting again)* I can't believe it!

JASON   Look, it happens all the time.

BRAD   Yeah, but not to *me.*

JASON   So big deal. You'll get a little heat from the principal's office. Since this is your first time it won't go on your record, and they probably won't even tell your parents.

BRAD   I could care less about my record, and I'm sure I can come up with some good excuses if my folks find out. *That's* not what I'm ticked about.

JASON   Then what is it? *(Pausing, then thinking he's figured it out)* Are you upset because you did something *wrong?*

BRAD   Wrong? Are you kidding? There's nothing wrong with cheating. Everybody does it. I just can't believe I was dumb enough to get *caught. That's* what's wrong.

★★★

Discussion Starters

1. Have you ever been caught doing something you shouldn't be doing? How did you feel? Did you ever do it again? Why or why not?

2. What determines whether an action such as stealing or cheating is right or wrong? Why do you think some people have no sense of right or wrong? How do you change that attitude?

3. How would you define the word "sin"? Do you believe that people are basically good or bad? Explain. Look up the following Bible verses: Genesis 8:21; Jeremiah 17:9-10; and Psalm 1:1. What do they say about the nature of human beings?

Zealous

— — — — — — — ☆ — — — — — — —

Topic: *Christian growth*

The Scene

A father speaks with his son about the son's zealous nature.

Characters

FATHER
MARK

★★★

(At home during a quiet evening. Father and Mark enter and sit down. Father is speaking with a very strained patience. Mark is wide-eyed and innocent.)

FATHER   All right, Son. Now, I know you mean well, and honestly there isn't anyone on the face of the earth who's more enthused about the changes in your life than I am.

MARK   I'm glad to hear that, Dad.

FATHER   When you chose to follow Jesus, your mother and I wept. It was an answer to our prayers.

MARK   I know, Dad. Your prayers made all the difference.

FATHER   That's what makes this so hard to do.

MARK   What's wrong?

FATHER   You're still young in your faith. Your enthusiasm is strong but . . . possibly misguided.

MARK   I've been studying my Bible every spare moment of my day.

FATHER   I know! It's inspiring. But I'm thinking about other, more practical examples.

MARK	Like what?
FATHER	Like the record-burnings you did in the back yard.
MARK	Great, huh? We have to purge our sinful habits with fire, Dad.
FATHER	I understand that. But you nearly asphyxiated the dog. The smoke from burning vinyl can be toxic, you know.
MARK	I'll be more careful about that.
FATHER	Thank you. But that wasn't the only thing, Mark.
MARK	Oh?
FATHER	Yes... *(Suddenly, with much feeling)* You burned *my* records!
MARK	It was for your own good, Dad. Those records weren't spiritually healthy for you.
FATHER	Perry Como? Percy Faith? The Baja Marimba band?
MARK	Haven't you ever read about backward-masking?
FATHER	Look, all I'm saying is, use wisdom and discretion in your faith.
MARK	And leave your records alone.
FATHER	Bingo.
MARK	Okay. If you want to endanger your Christianity...
FATHER	I'll take that chance.

(Father exits.)

MARK	I guess I shouldn't tell him about the bumper stickers I put all over his car.

(He exits.)

Discussion Starters

1. Was Mark right or wrong in what he did to his father's records? Explain. Was his *attitude* right or wrong? Explain.

2. The father advised his son to use "wisdom and discretion" in his faith. What do you think he meant by that?

3. Notice Paul's thoughts about a certain group in Romans 10:2 (NIV). What does he mean by "zeal" without "knowledge"? Is it possible to be extremely zealous for something without really understanding it? How might that same phrase be used for some Christians? How might the opposite be true: knowledgeable Christians who lack zeal? Do you know any in either category? Explain. Do you fit in either category? Explain.

Index of Topics

Bible Study Series

Give Your Teenagers a Solid Faith Foundation That Lasts a Lifetime!

Here are the *essentials* of the Christian life—core values teenagers *must* believe to make good decisions now. . . and build an *unshakable* lifelong faith. Developed by youth workers like you. . . field-tested with *real* youth groups in *real* churches...here's the meat your kids *must* have to grow spiritually—presented in a fun, involving way!

Each 4-session, **Core Belief Bible Study Series** book lets you easily. . .

- •Lead deep, compelling, *relevant* discussions your kids won't want to miss. . .
- •Involve teenagers in exploring life-changing truths. . .
- •Ground your teenagers in God's Word. . . and
- •Help kids create healthy relationships with each other—and you!
- •**Plus you'll make an *eternal difference* in the lives of your kids** as you give them a solid faith foundation that stands firm on God's Word.

Here are the Core Belief Bible Study Series titles already available...

Senior High Studies

Why **Being a Christian** Matters	0-7644-0883-6
Why **Creation** Matters	0-7644-0880-1
Why **God** Matters	0-7644-0874-7
Why **Jesus Christ** Matters	0-7644-0875-5
Why **Spiritual Growth** Matters	0-7644-0884-4
Why **Suffering** Matters	0-7644-0879-8
Why the **Bible** Matters	0-7644-0882-8
Why the **Holy Spirit** Matters	0-7644-0876-3
Why the **Spiritual Realm** Matters	0-7644-0881-X

Junior High/Middle School Studies

The Truth About **Being a Christian**	0-7644-0859-3
The Truth About **Creation**	0-7644-0856-9
The Truth About **God**	0-7644-0850-X
The Truth About **Jesus Christ**	0-7644-0851-8
The Truth About **Spiritual Growth**	0-7644-0860-7
The Truth About **Suffering**	0-7644-0855-0
The Truth About the **Bible**	0-7644-0858-5
The Truth About the **Holy Spirit**	0-7644-0852-6
The Truth About the **Spiritual Realm**	0-7644-0857-7

Order today from your local Christian bookstore, or write: Group Publishing, P.O. Box 485, Loveland, CO 80539.

Practical Resources for Your Youth Ministry

Fun & Rowdy

Here are teenagers' 25 favorite fun and rowdy Christian songs, each complete with quick, on-the-spot activities that involve kids directly in the music and message of each tune.

And whether you play guitar or piano—you're covered! You get both piano accompaniment and guitar chords.

Youth workers, Sunday school teachers, youth worship leaders, and youth choirs will all applaud these most-requested, raise-the-rafters, upbeat songs.
1-55945-475-X

Group's Best Discussion Launchers for Youth Ministry

You want your kids to open up. To get past giving you the "right" answers to share what they're *really* thinking and feeling.

No problem. Here's the definitive collection of Group's best-ever discussion launchers!

You'll get **thought-provoking questions** kids can't *resist* answering. . . **compelling quotes** that *demand* a response. . . and **quick activities** that pull kids into an experience they can't *wait* to talk about.

Add zing to your youth meetings. . . revive meetings that are drifting off-track. . . and comfortably approach sensitive topics like AIDS, war, cults, gangs, suicide, dating, parents, self-image, and more.
0-7644-2023-2

You-Choose-the-Ending Skits for Youth Ministry

Stephen Parolini

There's nothing quite as boring as "Sunday school skits" with endings you can see a mile away. Your kids hate them. You hate them. *So quit doing them!*

Instead, try these 19 hot-topic skits *guaranteed* to keep your kids on the edge of their seats—because each skit has **three possible endings!**

You can choose the ending. . . flip a coin. . . or let your teenagers vote. No matter which ending you pick, you'll get a great discussion going about a topic kids care about!

Skits require few actors. . . little or no rehearsal. . . and many skits get your audience involved, too, for maximum impact. Included: no-fail discussion questions!
1-55945-627-2

More Practical Resources for Your Youth Ministry

Last Impressions: Unforgettable Closings for Youth Meetings

Here's a collection of over 170 of Group's best-ever low-prep (or no-prep!) meeting closings...and each is tied to a thought-provoking Bible passage! You'll be ready with thoughtful...affirming...issue-oriented...high-energy...prayerful...and servanthood closings—on a moment's notice!

1-55945-629-9

Ready-to-Use Letters for Youth Ministry

Tom Tozer

These 110 already-written letters cover practically any situation that arises in youth ministry. And the included IBM-compatible computer disk makes adapting these letters quick and easy. You'll save hours of administrative time with this handy resource!

1-55945-692-2

Get Real: Making Core Christian Beliefs Relevant to Teenagers

Mike Nappa, Amy Nappa & Michael D. Warden

Here are the 24 Bible truths that Christian teenagers *must* know to survive in an unbelieving world. Included: proven strategies for effectively communicating these core Christian beliefs into the chaotic, fast-paced youth culture.

1-55945-708-2

Growing Close

These 150 practical, quick ideas help break the ice when teenagers don't know each other and break down cliques that often form in groups. A must-have resource for youth workers, coaches, camp directors, and Christian school teachers.

1-55945-709-0

Order today from your local Christian bookstore, or write: Group Publishing, P.O. Box 485, Loveland, CO 80539.